Help! My Kid Likes Fanfiction

The Christian Parent's Guide to a Mystery-clad Story Form

D. T. Powell

Ebook ISBN-13: 978-1-967586-00-4
Paperback ISBN-13: 978-1-967586-01-1

Cover design by: D. T. Powell

Printed in the United States of America

Additional resources for
Christian Fanfiction writers can
be found at dtpowellwrites.com

Table of Contents

Isaiah 6:8 (KJV)

Also I heard the voice of the Lord, saying,
Whom shall I send, and who will go for us?
Then said I, Here am I; send me.

For Heyna and Meli.

Give your words to God, and
He will refine them into something incredible.

Part 1

The Purpose of This Book

Part of a parent's responsibility is keeping their child safe. But another part is helping them become adults.

All reading—Original Fiction, Fanfiction, and Non-fiction—comes with potential risks and rewards.

This book isn't here to tell you whether Fanfiction will ultimately be beneficial for your child(ren). Only you can make that determination with God's help.

The purpose of this book is to provide information, so you are better equipped to deal with this topic if and when it arises. It dispels the mystery surrounding Fanfiction and helps make the subject one you can confidently and knowledgeably discuss with your kids. It gives you positive and negative factors to consider. And it presents my personal connection with Fanfiction and how it's effected my Christian Faith.

If, after reading this book, spending time with God and talking with your kids and spouse, you decide Fanfiction isn't something that would help your family, then this book has been successful. If you read this book, talk with God and your family, and decide Fanfiction is likely to be valuable and helpful with proper guidelines in place, this book has also succeeded. The important thing is that you've put in the effort to determine whether Fanfiction is a beneficial place for your family to spend time.

Part 2

The Basics of Fanfiction

What Is Fanfiction?

The simplest definition of Fanfiction is: content created using previously published characters or settings; sometimes abbreviated "fanfic" or "fic."

Fanfiction takes worlds and characters others have made and allows another group or individual to create stories for those characters and worlds. It makes published fiction accessible in a unique way. Through Fanfiction, a person who loves a book, film, TV show, game, play, radio drama, etc. can spend even more time with the story and characters they value without having to rehash the same content ad nauseum.

How does Fanfiction compare to Original Fiction?

Original Fiction is a piece of fiction not based on existing fictional content (i.e. anything you could legally purchase in a bookstore or at an online retailer). This term can also be applied to a piece of fiction that retells a classic story or uses characters or elements from fiction that is currently in the Public Domain. Traditionally published books as well as Independently (Indie) Published books, movies, games, etc. are considered Original.

What's Similar?

Like Original Fiction, Fanfiction contains plot, setting, and characters. Though some fics may be lighter or heavier on one or more of those elements than most published Original Fiction.

Additionally, many seasoned Fanfiction writers edit their work before publishing it, and some exhibit writing skills just as refined as Original Fiction authors.

As with Original Fiction, anyone can write Fanfiction, no matter their age, social standing, nationality, gender, financial status, etc.

Another similarity is that Fanfiction also offers a wide variety of content. In larger fandoms, there's something out there for everyone. Unfortunately, that means there's both good and not so good content out there. As with Original Fiction, it's important to learn how to find good content and weed out everything else.

Original Fiction readers are passionate about the stories they love. So are Fanfiction readers. I'd go so far as to say Fanfiction readers are even more passionate than Original Fiction readers—which is probably why they're reading Fanfiction in the first place.

What's Different?

There is way more Original Fiction out there than Fanfiction. Although Fanfiction as a concept has been around longer than most people know, Original Fiction is far more prevalent.

On the whole, Fanfiction does tend to be lower quality than Original Fiction. Due to the nonexistent barrier to entry for the Fanfiction space, literally anyone with internet access can post a story for public consumption. And although many Fanfiction writers use early readers (Betas), many do not. Some unfortunately don't even proofread their work before uploading it.

Another difference between Original Fiction and Fanfiction is that Original Fiction carries with it certain expectations. Consumers expect Original Fiction to offer something new every time a book, episode, or story installment comes out. Fanfiction is held to the opposite standard. Many readers come to Fanfiction to see something familiar, not to be pulled into a world they don't know. Yes, Fanfiction readers expect innovation, but they often expect it to remain contained within familiar territory.

What kinds of Fanfiction are there?

Fanfiction can be categorized in multiple ways. The most popular is by Fandom.

A Fandom is an individual intellectual property (i.e. Sherlock Holmes, *Little Women*, *Beowulf*). The word "fandom" can also be used as a reference to the individuals who like and interact with a body of published content.

Everywhere Fanfiction is available, it's grouped into categories based on which intellectual property it's associated with.

Within Fandoms, fics are categorized by their Rating.

A rating is a way to indicate the intensity of the material within a fanfic; somewhat akin to the TV rating system, but with noticeable differences; ratings are assigned by the writer of the fic and may not be accurate one hundred percent of the time.

Looking at a fic's Rating can be very helpful, as long as the writer of the fic has rated their piece appropriately. Ratings can indicate whether a story contains explicit material, heavy gore and violence, frequent foul language, same-sex romance, or other potential content concerns.

Another method for categorizing Fanfiction is by Type.

There are four significant Types of fanfic: Canon Compliant, Post-Canon, Canon Divergent, and Alternate Universe (AU).

In Fanfiction, Canon is material designated as part of the official timeline of a specific intellectual property. So, a Canon Compliant fic is a work that does not alter canon material. These types of fics take place before or during the source material's official timeline.

An example of a Canon Compliant fic is a story taking place between two of The Chronicles of Narnia books and not changing any of the previous or subsequent events, characters, or settings. Something like following Lucy Pevensie as she watches her father leave for the war. This story would be set between *The Magician's Nephew* and *The Lion, the Witch, and the Wardrobe*, but it would not change anything already established by C. S. Lewis.

Post-Canon fics begin after the timeline represented in canon material ends. For example, a piece that takes place after the second part of Bunyan's *Pilgrim's Progress, Christiana's Story* and does not alter the events, settings, or characters already included in the story would be Post-Canon.

A Canon Divergent fic uses at least one canon event as a foundation but differs thereafter on key points. An example of a Canon Divergent fic is a story that explores what would happen if, in Tolkien's *The Fellowship of the Ring*, someone besides Frodo was chosen to be the ringbearer after the Council of Elrond. A story like this would look at how diverging or "branching off" from canon would alter the story as a whole.

Lastly, an Alternate Universe fic (often abbreviated AU) builds from canon but changes foundational elements of the world and/or characters. An example of an AU fic is a story that takes Madeline L'Engle's *A Wrinkle in Time* and sets it in Southeast Asia instead of the U. S.

There are many other ways to categorize Fanfiction, but these three are the most popular and widely referenced.

Why does my kid like Fanfiction?

That's a wonderful question to ask your child. Finding out why your kid, specifically, likes Fanfiction can tell you a lot about them as a person and how they relate to and view the world around them.

Generally speaking, there are many good and/or innocent reasons people like Fanfiction.

- Finding more content that includes a beloved fictional person or place
- Correcting canon's perceived wrongs
- Ending a story that was never officially finished
- Getting to see a favorite couple spend time together
- Viewing a fictional world from a new perspective
- Practicing a second language in a low-stress environment
- Finding new favorite stories and writers
- Practicing Biblical self-reflection and evaluation
- Learning more about writing and story structure
- And many more

However, just as with Original Fiction, there are also unsavory reasons for reading Fanfiction. Many of these involve explicit, violent, or otherwise destructive content. Fics that dwell on cruelty and blood lust, showcase unsavory wish fulfillment, explore sexual promiscuity, glorify unbiblical lifestyles, romanticize self-harm and abuse, and promote humanistic worldviews are all too easy to find. Knowing your child and their sensitivities is just as important when screening Fanfiction as it is when evaluating whether a specific piece of Original Fiction is appropriate for them.

Chances are, a kid who is reading Fanfiction is doing it because they love the source material the fic(s) is based on. But it never hurts to dig deeper and make them think about why they like certain stories more than others.

Where is my kid finding Fanfiction?

Probably a website. They may have landed there because of a search engine, or a friend sent them a link. It's also possible they stumbled across it through social media posts or heard about it via word of mouth.

Some Fanfiction websites have the option to download fics either chapter by chapter or all at once. In that case, if your child has access to any devices, they could also be reading Fanfiction while offline. Reading while offline may indicate an intent to conceal reading habits, but it could just as easily be a matter of convenience. If a child is frequently offline and wants to read an engaging fanfic without connecting to the internet, downloading it is a good solution.

There are multiple websites dedicated to Fanfiction. The two most popular ones are Archive of Our Own (AO3), and Fanfiction.net (FFN). Each site has features the other does not.

For example, FFN allows users to directly message each other, while AO3 limits user interaction to public comments.

FFN allows writers to select the fandom, rating, genre, and main characters of their fics. Officially, it does not allow explicit content, however users still post it in the hopes the admins won't notice.

AO3 also employs a rating system and prompts writers to select at least one fandom. But from there, writers are able to tag their fic in any way they like. AO3 also allows explicit content and provides a rating for it (Explicit fics are rated E).

FFN's system makes it easy to find fics by genre and rating, but difficult to see what the fic is rated for. AO3 makes it much easier to know whether a fic contains something that might better be steered clear of.

In addition to AO3 and FFN, Fanfiction is also available on sites like Wattpad, Webnovel, and fandom-specific sites.

Who writes and reads Fanfiction?

Anyone who wants to.

Most Fanfiction sites require users to be thirteen or older, but it's easy to check a box and move on, regardless of your true age. However, Fanfiction posted online is only a portion of the Fanfiction that gets written. Some Fanfiction writers never share their work with others.

From kids just learning what a story is to seasoned adults who've experienced thousands of stories, and everyone in between, Fanfiction writers and readers are all unique and bring interesting and diverse perspectives to already published worlds, characters, and stories.

Part 3

The Pros and Cons of Fanfiction

Is Fanfiction legal?

People have asked this question frequently over the past several decades.

The short answer is somewhere between yes and no.

Fanfiction's legitimacy as a writing form has been challenged throughout the years, but it remains a popular medium for many thousands of writers across the globe.

The general consensus is that Fanfiction is acceptable as long as the writer does not profit from it monetarily.

There are a few other limitations. First, some creators do not want Fanfiction published based on their work. Should an individual creator make this request, it falls to Fanfiction writers to respect that request and refrain from publishing or otherwise sharing Fanfiction based on that creator's works or worlds. If a Fanfiction site is aware of a creator request, they will make it known to the site users.

Second, some Fanfiction websites do not allow work that includes non-historical figures. Generally speaking, Fanfiction that includes non-fictional people is known as RPF (Real Person Fiction). Some Fanfiction sites do not allow RPF that involves living or recently living individuals. For example, Pop stars and current celebrities would be off-limits. But writing about people from the past may be considered acceptable. Historical figures like George Washington, Genghis Khan, or Johannes Kepler could be perfectly fine to include in a work of Fanfiction, as long as the story connects to a

Fandom. Some sites set this limitation to prevent getting into legal trouble.

Third, most Fanfiction sites do not allow writers to quote copyrighted content. This includes song lyrics, movie dialogue, books passages, video game scripts, etc. Sites give users this limitation to keep the site from being sued. Quotations from Public Domain content, however, are perfectly acceptable.

What concerns are associated with reading and writing Fanfiction?

Many parents choose to screen the Original Fiction their child engages with. A parent(s) with this priority will likely also screen their child's Fanfiction reading choices.

There are concerns inherent in allowing children to interact with any form of media. Just as with Original Fiction, there are potential pitfalls involved with reading Fanfiction.

The first reason to screen and/or limit a child's Fanfiction reading is exposure to unwanted content. Christian parents may have multiple things they don't want their kids exposed to. These include, but are not limited to the following:

- Explicit, violent, vulgar, or otherwise inappropriate material

- Age-inappropriate content
- Unbiblical worldviews portrayed positively
- Political propaganda
- Stories without purpose
- Exceptionally poor grammar

As with Original Fiction, many Fanfiction pieces contain explicit scenes. In the fanfic world, however, this content is more likely to be disclosed ahead of time. With content ratings and tags for Smut (detailed sexual content), Slash (same-sex romance), Non-con (non-consensual sex), Under-age characters (usually used in conjunction with sexual situations), all forms of violence, and any other potentially objectionable situation, knowing whether to avoid a piece of Fanfiction can be quite easy. As long as the writer has appropriately tagged and rated their work.

What isn't likely to be tagged is bad grammar. Nonsensical plots are something else parents may need to look further to find.

But the body of the work isn't the only place readers may run across unwanted content. Cursing and other rough language may also appear in comments left on published Fanfiction. Some sites hide comments and reviews by default, but others do not.

Another potential concern involved with children engaging with Fanfiction is unmonitored communication with strangers. Some sites allow users to exchange direct messages while others only allow public discourse. Either way, if a child is reading Fanfiction from a more popular Fandom, it's likely they'll interact with people they don't know, even if only on a cursory level. The majority of Fanfiction readers have no ill-will or other nefarious intentions toward fellow Fanfiction readers or writers.

However, encountering Trolls and Scammers is inevitable, given time.

A Troll is a user who harasses others. Harassment enacted by a troll is called Trolling. Harassment may ensue over literally anything—fandom choice, fic preferences, username, age, or whatever else the Troll feels like making comments about. Troll comments are best ignored, blocked, and reported to site administrators.

Scammers contact others under false pretenses, usually with the ultimate goal of taking financial and/or emotional advantage of the person they're contacting. If you or your child is contacted via a Fanfiction site by someone offering paid services, that person is a scammer. Do not interact with them, block their account, and report them to site administrators.

Especially in today's age of AI chatbots that can spit out whole volumes of cordially worded text instantly, if it isn't clear whether someone is a scammer, there are two main options. Either ignore them completely or ask them targeted questions without revealing personal information. Which course of action to take is a choice each person has to make. It would be advisable for parents to discuss with their children what the family protocol is for communicating with scammers online.

What are the benefits of reading or writing Fanfiction?

Find Motivation to Read

Reading boosts empathy, vocabulary, communication skills, imagination, attention span, critical thinking, and more.

Fanfiction specifically can become a bridge for reluctant readers by giving them a world and characters they already know and love. It also affords a place of familiarity for seasoned readers who may not have the time or energy to invest in an unfamiliar fictional place and its people. Some readers may also find it easier to pay attention to a world and characters they're already familiar with.

It's one thing to create or spend time in a wholly original world. It's another to visit a world someone else built. Fanfiction affords a unique mix of both elements. Readers get to see, not just the places and people they know, but new situations, settings, and characters, written by others who love the source material just as much as the reader.

Having several elements of a story already cemented in place makes imagining new pieces less challenging for people who don't spend regular time reading. That also means the reader gets to practice reading and exercising imagination in a lower stress environment.

Through Fanfiction, a reluctant or less skilled reader can strengthen their ability to comprehend and analyze the written word without having to step into unknown fictional territory before they're ready.

Fanfiction is also free and easy to find. No need to even leave the house, unless you don't have internet access.

Find Motivation to Write

Writing is a skill. Yes, some people are born with more innate writing talent than others, but that doesn't mean someone with a lower initial skill level shouldn't write. Nor does it mean writing cannot be learned or improved with practice. Even the most naturally talented writers spend a lot of time refining their craft and trying new things.

A beginner writer may feel overwhelmed at the prospect of creating a wholly original world and characters on top of figuring out what on earth is going to happen within their story. Fanfiction offers a place they can start without having to do a ton of world building up front. Instead of spending months—or even years—designing a world and its people, cultures, geography, economy, religions, etc. Fanfiction allows writers to dive right into practicing story and storytelling.

There's always room in Fanfiction for writers to world build and write new characters, but a brand-new writer who isn't willing or able to start with world and character creation is free to not focus on those elements right away.

Seasoned writers who also have to balance full-time or part-time work, caring for family members, health needs, and any number of other responsibilities are another prime candidate for writing Fanfiction, because it can be much less time consuming than Original Fiction.

Writers of all skill levels take time to try something they've never done before. Fanfiction can be a place where writers exercise their writing muscles in new ways. Tackle a unique story format, attempt a different point of view, write in a new genre, practice structuring sentences differently—all this and more are possible to do in Fanfiction without spending a lot of preparation time.

Writing Fanfiction can also be a place writers work through personal struggles or even questions of Faith. Working with fictional people they already know lends a sense of security and confidence that writing Original Fiction doesn't always provide. Within Fanfiction, a writer can examine what they believe and why and see both the rewards and consequences of those beliefs play out on page.

Build Social Skills

The Fanfiction community is large and diverse. Readers and writers vary in age, nationality, geographical location, religion, political views, fandom preferences, favorite characters, and so much more.

Fanfiction is a place where communication with people around the globe is not only possible but highly likely. Spending time in such a diverse environment allows participants to learn how to interact with both people who agree and disagree with them on key points. It also provides a space where kids (and adults) can learn how to establish and maintain personal boundaries.

If a parent decides their child is mature enough to navigate the Fanfiction space independently, there's merit in talking with that child about what to do in certain situations and how best to handle both friendly and unfriendly interactions with strangers online.

With so many differing opinions on fiction and individual elements of every fictional world and story ever created, it's a good idea to know how to maintain a "just keep scrolling" mindset. Anyone actively on social media understands that others will say things they disagree with. Offending comments may also be just plain false, ignorant, or even hateful. Whatever the case, attempting to counter every error-riddled opinion will only earn contempt. Spending time in the Fanfiction space can be a way to exercise discernment when choosing which verbal battles to publicly participate in.

Exercise Faith

Yes, you read that right. Fanfiction can be a place where we, as Christians, learn better how to effectively exercise our Faith in everyday life. Fanfiction readers get opportunities to use discernment, not just when it comes to deciding whether a story will be helpful for them to read, but when they're tempted to be swept up in a wild rush of unhelpful emotion or believe it's all right to do something unbiblical as long as it's helping someone else.

Fanfiction is a place where readers see people they already know and care about doing things they may or may not agree with. Moments of moral disagreement with a character or story are especially useful in helping us understand what we truly believe.

When a stranger acts unbiblically, it's easy to say, "that's wrong" and walk away unfazed. But what happens when it's your friend or family member? Can you so easily admit when wrong occurs? How do you respond to that wrong? How do you speak truth without destroying an important relationship?

It isn't so easy to pass immediate judgment on a situation where the people involved are important to you. But dealing with tough situations is an unfortunate fact of life in a fallen world, so it's wise to learn how to handle them well when they do happen.

People who interact with fiction in any form get attached to fictional characters. Sometimes that happens instantly. Other connections form over time. Just as with anything else, the most potent attachments we have to fictional people are the ones we maintain and cultivate regularly. Reading Fanfiction as a Christian challenges us to view our fictional connections through the lens of Scripture. It provides opportunity for us to ask ourselves who we view as the ultimate authority in our lives. Who we listen to, no matter what. If we determine to think Biblically during our Fanfiction reading (or writing) time, it helps prepare us to remain grounded when facing difficult situations involving family or other loved ones. Because now we've practiced how to think and act when someone we care very much about and have a longstanding connection with acts unbiblically.

Spending time in Fanfiction makes this kind of self-examination and reflection more possible by providing new events and situations not previously available. It allows an element of surprise and organic development that just isn't possible once someone has read, seen, or heard the entirety of a fictional world's Canon content.

This possibility for growth expands exponentially when writing Fanfiction comes into play. Because now, we're no longer bound by what someone else has written. The universe is entirely open to us, and literally anything is possible, if we take the time to write it. No matter the fictional situation, we can choose to use it as an opportunity to practice Biblical thinking.

How can my kid stay safe while reading Fanfiction?

Should you determine your child is properly equipped to handle interacting with Fanfiction in an online environment, there are multiple things they need to remember as a minor in a public space.

1. Not everyone online has good intentions. Never share any of the following:
   + Passwords
   + Personal information, including:
     - Legal name
     - Age
     - Gender
     - Address
     - State/Country of residence
     - Phone number
     - Email address
     - Picture/Appearance
     - Contact info for other communication apps
     - School name or address
     - Vehicle or house description

- Details about family members
- Names of pets
- Favorite color, book, show, movie, etc.
- Financial status
- Anything else a stranger might use to locate or identify you

+ Current location
+ Social media accounts

2. Never take rude comments personally. The person sending unkind message may just be having a bad day. No need to make anyone's day worse (including yours) by escalating the situation. However, there are also people in this world who love to make others miserable. Letting bullies and trolls make you angry or upset only encourages them. Should someone become hostile on a Fanfiction site, the best things to do are:

- Ignore them.
- Report the comment or message to site admins.
- Block the user who made the comment or sent the message.
- Delete the comment or message if necessary. You may wish to keep the comment or message until site admins look into it.
- Minors: Tell a parent or guardian.
- Do not reply.

3. Always behave respectfully. Fanfiction sites have rules for a reason. Follow them.

4. Exposure to unwanted content will happen. Encourage your child to tell you if they run across something unsavory. This creates an opportunity to Biblically discuss whatever content they've stumbled into and promotes an environment of trust and security.

As with Original Fiction and Non-fiction, the content represented in Fanfiction varies widely. Knowing your child and what is constructive and detrimental for them will be a significant help when determining if a particular piece of Fanfiction is appropriate.

Part 4

The Connection Between Faith and Fanfiction

Why write Fanfiction?

When I was twelve, God brought a story into my life that changed the way I looked at myself and the world around me.

Having grown up in a Christian home and accepted Christ as my Saviour at the age of four, my Faith was something I knew quite a bit about. But though I actively tried to do what was right and experienced conviction when I did wrong, my relationship with God was distant and sterile.

From the beginning, my parents instilled in me a love of fiction and reading, so by the time I became a Christian, even though I couldn't read yet, story was an integral part of my existence. To this day, fiction is a vital piece of who I am and how I understand and perceive truth.

By the time I turned nine, I had fallen prey to selfishness and pride. It had come to the point that my father said to me very clearly, "The world does not revolve around you."

Those words stuck with me, but I didn't know what to do about them—or if they even needed to be addressed. My life was fine as it was. I was a good kid, never got into trouble at school, listened, and learned at church, and didn't flagrantly disobey my parents. In my limited view of myself, I thought I was doing quite well.

Then God arranged a single moment in my life that altered my course completely—a meeting only He knew the significance of.

During my family's weekly trip to the local library, my mother found something in the kids' fiction section she thought I would like. (I'm about to date myself here.) A VHS tape with images of space and interesting looking people on the cover.

We checked out the tape, and I watched it at the earliest opportunity. That story gripped me in a way I still can't explain. As I watched first that tape and then five more, I got to see what it meant to fight for good and protect others. I grew to appreciate the heroes and sympathized with them.

But it wasn't the good guys who so thoroughly captured my attention. It was the villain.

And I hated him. Vehemently. My hatred escalated to the point that I said out loud, "I hope he dies."

When the last episode of that story arrived, and the villain didn't make it out alive, I was ecstatic. The man I'd hated for months had finally gotten what I'd single-handedly determined he deserved. His sentence had been carried out, and his sins judged in the harshest way my nine-year-old heart could imagine.

For a while, I was content. I spent time watching those six VHS tapes over and over, and I always found satisfaction in that villain's death.

Then God arranged a second meeting.

Our library system acquired the next part of that story.

When I found out there were now twelve tapes to watch, I jumped at the chance to see the next six. What new adventures might the heroes have, especially now that their nemesis was gone?

Several new episodes passed, and I was thoroughly invested in this second section of the story. Until someone I recognized all too well re-appeared. The villain who'd died at the end of part one was somehow back for part two. I was so angry, I said out loud, "Why couldn't he just stay dead?" His return was never truly explained, but what little anyone (including the writer) knew is that he was raised from the dead.

With building rage, I watched as this awful man once again stepped in and made everything so much worse for the heroes—who now had two villains to deal with instead of one.

But as the story unfolded, something I never anticipated happened.

The man I hated so much . . . changed. He turned from evil and became a force for good.

I did not know how to process this. How could someone I hated so thoroughly become a friend of the heroes?

How was I supposed to think of him now?

I was at an impasse. I wanted to hate him. I wanted to dismiss him—tell him to leave and never come back. But I knew I shouldn't.

I did a lot of soul searching over the next weeks and months, and I realized why I hated this man.

He reminded me of myself.

In that moment, I understood that God saw my sin as something hideous and unlovable, but despite what I'd done, He still chose to redeem me—chose to save me when I asked Him to. He didn't turn me away. He made me His child—His friend.

That was the moment my salvation gained personal meaning for me, and I've never lost the joy of it.

I have never looked at that character, that former villain, the same way since. For me, he's become a memorial of God's unfailing mercy. And a friend. Whenever I spend time with him, I remember what God has done for me.

I spent the next ten years looking for a way to show the world even just a hint of the wonder I've known since that moment. I tried music, and every visual art I could think of. I even went to college to get an art degree. But I was summarily dismissed from the program because I wasn't good enough. So, I earned a B.A. in business instead.

After graduation, I spent four months unemployed. During that time, God brought my focus to the one medium I'd never thought to try.

Writing.

So, I picked up a pen.

And I've never put it down.

The first story I wrote was a novel-length Fanfic, featuring the fictional people God has used to work so powerfully in my life. Since then, I've written five novel-length fics and forty short stories in the same world. Each one reminds me of who God is and what He's done for me.

I write fearless Original Christian fiction and Fanfiction in multiple genres. My work often tackles difficult subjects because I believe God can do the impossible, even redeem the most darkened of souls.

Can Fanfiction be "Christian"?

God says Christians are "the light of the world." (Matt. 5:14, KJV) He instructs us to let our "light so shine before men, that they may see your good works and glorify your Father which is in heaven." (Matt. 5:16, KJV) He also says we are "the salt of the earth." (Matt. 5:13, KJV)

Salt and light are potent. They can bring healing to the sick; expose wounds so they can be treated; chase away darkness and disease; communicate joy and hope to those who have seen only despair and sorrow for much too long. Salt and light are meant to be shared.

1 Peter 1:15 & 16 (KJV) says, "But as he which hath called you is holy, so be ye holy in all manner of conversation; Because it is written, Be ye holy; for I am holy."

We are to be holy, consecrated, dedicated, or set apart to God.

1 Peter goes on to tell us why we ought to be set apart. Because we "were not redeemed with [...] silver and gold. [...] but with the precious blood of Christ". (1 Peter 1:18 & 19, KJV) God didn't use money or goods to purchase our redemption. He offered the blood of His own Son, Jesus the Christ. If that isn't a payment worth being grateful for, I don't know what is.

My Fanfiction work isn't inherently Christian because it includes Christian characters. It isn't Christian because people pray and talk about God or explore Christian themes. It isn't Christian because there are no explicit scenes, overly gory moments, or on-page cursing. Although all those things are typically true of my work.

Too much "Christian" fiction focuses on whether

its characters "follow all the rules" of Christianity. And while I don't believe we need to throw out the lists, I do believe it's vital we look at how, why, and with what heart attitude we do what we do. I know from experience that someone can follow all the rules without understanding the why behind them.

God didn't create humanity so we could check off a list every day. He created us to have a relationship with Him. And that relationship ought to permeate every corner of life. From how we treat others at the grocery store, to the way we speak to our family members, to which stories we read and how we think about them. Each moment of every day is an opportunity to find out more about God, who He is, and who we are in light of God's Truth. It's also an opportunity to strengthen our relationship with Him.

As with writing Original Fiction, writing Fanfiction as a Christian isn't about converting the entire writing form into something sacred. It's holding out our hands to God and saying, "I'll go where You want me to go." As a Christian, I write the stories God directs me to. Whether those stories happen to be Original Fiction or Fanfiction doesn't matter. What does matter is that I have followed God's leading.

I seek the same guidance when reading. Everything I read, I measure against what God has said. As an adult secure in my Faith, I will at times read content that holds a significantly different worldview. The purpose of that is to better understand the people who disagree with me. It also humanizes those who hold opposing values and beliefs and keeps me from falling into the trap of looking down on others.

Even when I'm reading something that holds a view completely opposite mine, I keep God's Truth first in my mind and heart. Then, as I read, God's Truth sifts through lies and misconceptions, keeps me grounded, and helps me come to a Biblical perspective regarding what I'm reading and the people behind it.

The same is true when I find a story that holds pieces of Truth but has missed the bigger picture. Those stories whose author(s) cannot take Truth to its final conclusion are prime opportunities for me, as a Fanfiction writer, to pick up the story and bring it across the Finish Line of Truth.

Reading (whether it be Fanfiction or Original Fiction) is a wonderful way to exercise our Faith—to examine our responses to people, places, and events—to challenge ourselves with hard questions and invite God to help us find His answers.

So, while no story medium—including Fanfiction—is inherently "Christian" by the traditional definition, all stories can, and ought to be, filtered through the Truth of God's Word.

Is there a story in your life that's influenced you strongly for good or bad? Is there a story that's made a lasting impression on your child(ren)? Perhaps it's time to sit down with that story and see what happens when you look at it through the lens of God's Truth. Maybe God is already using fiction to focus your attention on Him and His Word.

Part 5

Glossary

Alternate Universe	a work which builds from canon but changes foundational elements of the world and/or characters; a form of fanfiction that deviates from canon, usually in a key aspect(s)
Anon	short for "anonymous"; this is a piece of fanfiction posted without a username attached to it; some sites allow this, and some do not
AO3	an abbreviation for archiveofourown.org, which is one of the most popular sites to post fanfiction
Beta	a person who reads a fanfic before it's posted; often, a beta will help with developmental/story elements as well as grammar and punctuation
Bookmark	a digital landmark allowing readers to find a fanfic they visited previously
Canon	material designated as part of the official timeline of a specific intellectual property
Canon Compliant	a work that does not alter canon material; canon compliant fics often occur during the fandom's already-established timeline; canon compliant fics can sometimes occur post-canon
Category	a term used on fanfiction.net to delineate types of canon sources; examples of categories include cartoons, movies, books, anime, etc.
Comment	a public response to a posted fanfic; AO3 (see "AO3") uses comments as their medium for reader feedback on posted fanfic; similar to a review (see "Review")

Concrit	an abbreviation for "constructive criticism"; a message from another fanfiction creator or reader that outlines how a piece of fanfiction can be improved; this may arrive in the form of a public comment or review or privately in a DM, depending on the site in use and the person giving the concrit
Cowriter	a person who assists a creator with writing a piece of fanfiction; often cowriters will contribute large portions of the written text as well as provide consultation on story elements
Crackfic	a piece of fanfiction that is meant to be ridiculous; sometimes crackfics work surprisingly well
Crossover	a piece of fanfiction that includes two or more fandoms (i.e. Winnie-the-Pooh and Journey to the Center of the Earth)
DLDR	short for "don't like, don't read"; this abbreviation is meant to notify or deter readers who do not care to read specific things; DLDR fics often have tags (see "Tag") or content warnings to inform readers of what is in a particular fic; DLDR can also be used as a way to indicate the writer is serious about the tags or warnings they included; DLDR fics often contain intense content and/or content not appropriate for kids
DocX	a document exchange system used by fanfiction.net to allow users to share files without providing personal information like email addresses or names

Fandom	an individual intellectual property (i.e. Sherlock Holmes, Little Women, Beowulf); can also be used as a reference to the individuals who like and interact with a body of published content
Fandom Blind	the state of being unfamiliar with a particular fandom's source material
Fanfiction	content created using previously published characters or settings; sometimes abbreviated "fanfic" or "fic"
Fave	a label assigned to a fic by a user to indicate it as a "favorite" story; this label is used by fanfiction.net
FFN	an abbreviation for the fanfiction website fanfiction.net
Filter	an option available on archiveofourown. org that allows users to include or exclude any type of content they choose; filter criteria may be based on fic rating, characters in the fic, tags, genre, fandom, etc.
Fix-it-fic	a piece of fanfiction that corrects a problem created by canon; common reasons for writing fix-it-fics include: a poorly done (or non-existent) ending to canon, an unjust or unneeded character death, a romantic relationship the writer didn't like, etc.
Flame	a belligerent or otherwise abusive comment or review left on a fanfic; flames are often posted anonymously and can sometimes be deleted; flames are sometimes posted by trolls (see "Trolls")
Fluff	a story or scene that focuses on cute or other low-conflict situations

Follow	a term used on fanfiction.net to indicate a user wants to receive notifications that a fic or other user has posted something new
Gary Stu	see "Mary Sue"
Gen Fic	a fic that focuses on platonic relationships like friendship, family dynamics, workplace connections, or other non-romantic relationships
Gender bending	writing a character with the gender opposite their canon portrayal (i.e. writing Little Women's Jo March as a man instead of a woman)
Headcanon	an individual person's views or theories about certain aspects of canon; sometimes referred to in terms such as, "I headcanon that X-thing happened off-screen, which is why Z-character responds this way"
Hit	an individual visit to a user's posted fanfic; similar to "View"
Kudos	a term used on archiveofourown.org to indicate another user liked a piece of posted fanfiction
Long fic	a fanfic that is novel-length or longer and cannot be easily read in one sitting; users have varying definitions of what constitutes a long-fic; some define it as any fic over 50k words, others say 100k+ or 200k+
Mary Sue	a character who is never presented as doing anything wrong; often someone everyone else in the story loves without exception, even when they do hurtful or unreasonable things; can be a sign of a poorly done self-insert (see "Self-Insert); Mary Sue is the female version of this, and Gary Stu is the male version

MSTing	a term for a fic where characters comment on another piece of fiction or their own canon; the term is an abbreviation for commenting on a film or book in a "Mystery Science Theater 3000" style; this kind of fanfic is often not allowed on fanfic sites, because it would necessitate quoting large portions of copyrighted material
Multi-chapter	a fic that contains multiple chapters; the opposite of a one-shot (see "One-shot")
Non-con	an abbreviation for Non-consensual sex; this tag sometimes appears alongside the Under-age tag (see "Under-age)
One-shot	a fic that contains a single chapter or installment; the opposite of a multi-chapter fic (see "Multi-chapter)
OOC	an abbreviation for "out of character"; the state of acting in a way inconsistent with who a person or character is
Original Character	a fan made character used in a work of fanfiction; sometimes abbreviated "OC"
Original Fiction	a piece of fiction that is not based on existing fictional content; can also be applied to a piece of fiction that retells a classic story or uses characters or elements from fiction that is currently in the Public Domain
Pairing	two or more characters "paired" together, usually romantically, by an individual fan or a collective fandom (see "Fandom"); related to "Ship"
Plot Bunny	a story line that originated as a departure from another fanfic piece
Podfic	a fanfic that is available to interact with in audio format

Post	a fanfic that has been published; the act of publishing an installment of fanfiction
Post Canon	a work that begins after the timeline represented in canon (see "Canon") material ends
Profile	a place users can go to find out more about an individual fanfiction writer or reader; different fanfiction sites have different formats for profile pages
Rating	a way to indicate the intensity of the material within a fanfic; somewhat akin to the TV rating system, but with noticeable differences; both AO3 and FFN include rating systems for fanfic content; ratings are assigned by the writer of the fic and may not be accurate one hundred percent of the time
Reaction Fic	similar to MSTing (see "MSTing") this type of fic includes characters' reactions to viewing or reading the story they appear in; this form of fanfiction is not allowed on some fanfic sites, since it would require quoting large portions of canon material
Review	a public response to a posted fanfic; FFN (see "FFN") uses reviews as their medium for public reader feedback on posted fanfic; similar to a comment (see "Comment")
RPF	an abbreviation for Real Person Fiction; fanfic that focuses on or includes non-fictional people; some fanfic sites do not allow RPF about non-historical figures; this is done to eliminate the possibility of legal repercussions
Salt and Light	a tag used by some Christian fanfiction writers to mark their fics as having been written from a Christian worldview or containing Christian themes

Script Format	a format that includes speaker tags, dialogue, and minimal stage directions; similar to a screenplay format; this fanfic form is not allowed on some fanfiction sites
Self-Insert	a writer's effort to put themselves into their story; sometimes abbreviated as "SI"
Ship	an abbreviation for "relationship"; the overwhelming majority of the time, the ships referred to in fanfic are romantic; ships can include any two or more characters; sometimes ships are tagged or noted by the author of an individual fanfic
Slash	a way to refer to fanfic that contains same-sex romantic pairings; sometimes indicated with labels such as M|M, MLM, F|F, etc.; also sometimes referred to as yaoi or yuri, especially in anime fandoms; slash fics often contain explicit material
Smut	a term for sexually descriptive or explicit content
Song Fic	a fanfic written based on a song; often includes song lyrics in the body of the fic; some fanfic sites do not allow this fanfic form, since it requires quoting significant portions of copyrighted material
SPaG	an abbreviation for "Spelling, Punctuation, and Grammar"
Summary	a brief explanation of what a fanfic is about
Tag	labels added to a fic by its author; these can be content or theme related, refer to characters or character relationships, indicate the fandom(s) a fic is connected with, or be anything else the author wants; tags are especially useful when filtering out fics a reader does not want to see or narrowing search results to fics a reader is interested in

Troll	a user who harasses others; harassment enacted by a troll is called trolling; trolling can take various forms (i.e. frequent nonsensical or rude comments/ reviews, posting flames, spamming a user's private messages, actively encouraging other users to avoid or harass a user, etc.)
Under-age	a tag to indicate a fanfic includes sexual situations that involve characters under the age of 18; this tag sometimes appears alongside the Non-can tag (see "Non-con")
Update	a new installment of a posted fanfic
Username	a way to refer to a specific fanfic writer or reader; sometimes abbreviated "UN"; a way to keep from sharing personal information online by using a moniker other than a person's legal name
View	a unit of measure used to indicate that someone has accessed a user's posted fic or chapter; some fanfiction sites track views of individual chapters, others only track views of a fic as a whole; similar to "Hit"

Acknowledgments

I would not be who I am today had God not brought certain stories into my life. It's because He arranged the perfect meetings with several fictional people that I'm even writing anything aside from grocery lists. This little book is just one small informational foray into something that's been an incredible help to me for the majority of my life.

Reader, if you've come this far, thank you for sticking with me and looking at what I have to say about this often-neglected topic.

About The Author

D. T. Powell, author of the critically acclaimed, award-winning novel With Mercy's Eyes, has delved into difficult subjects through fiction for over a decade. Her work in both fanfiction and original fiction showcases how God's persistent light shines even through the darkest of moments. Her original short fiction has appeared in Writer's Digest and various short story collections from small presses. Also, her many top-quality book reviews publish quarterly in Clean Fiction Magazine. She enjoys reading, playing pickleball, and the occasional video game. You can find her online as dtill359. Her favorite verse is Psalm 126:5, "They that sow in tears shall reap in joy."

More Books and Short Fiction by D. T. Powell

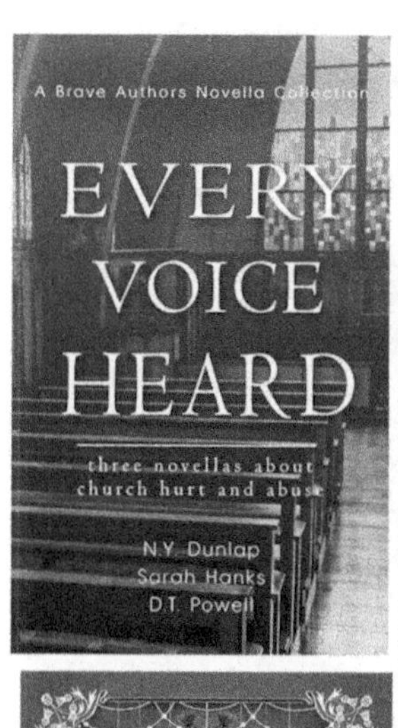

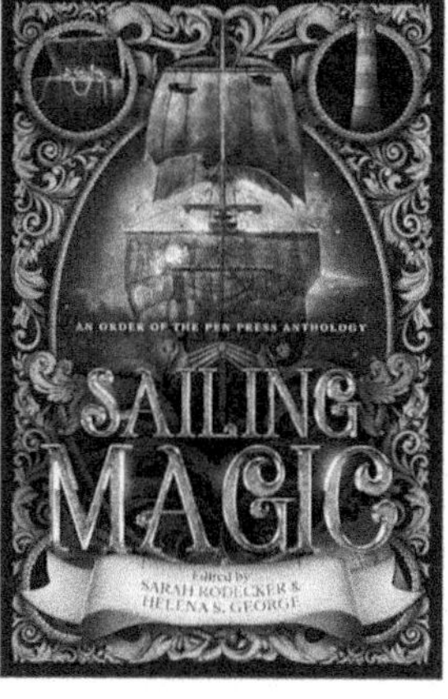

Get two free short stories from D. T. Powell at dtpowellwrites.com

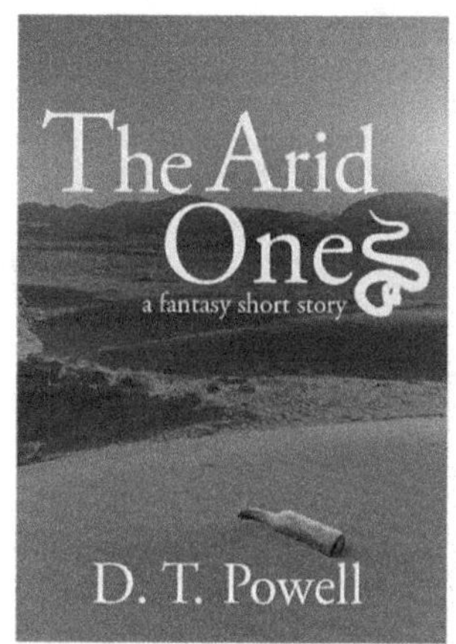

www.ingramcontent.com/pod-product-compliance
Lightning Source LLC
La Vergne TN
LVHW010942110826
845149LV00013B/2718

* 9 7 8 1 9 6 7 5 8 6 0 1 1 *